The Brothers Grimm

Little Red Riding Hood

Retold by Jenny Dooley

Stage 1 Pupil's Book

Express Publishing

Published by Express Publishing

Liberty House, New Greenham Park, Newbury,
Berkshire RG19 6HW
Tel.: (0044) 1635 817 363
Fax: (0044) 1635 817 463
e-mail: inquiries@expresspublishing.co.uk
http://www.expresspublishing.co.uk

© Jenny Dooley, 2003

Design and Illustration © Express Publishing, 2003

Colour Illustrations: Terry Wilson

Music by Ted & Taz © Express Publishing, 2003

First published 2003
Published in this edition 2008
Third impression 2010

Made in EU

All rights reserved. No part of this publication may be reproduced, stored in a retrieval system or transmitted in any form, or by any means, electronic, photocopying or otherwise, without the prior written permission of the publishers.

This book is not meant to be changed in any way.

ISBN 978-1-84466-482-5

CONTENTS

Little Red Riding Hood .... p. 4

Song: Red Riding Hood .... p. 16

Little Red Riding Hood .... p. 18

Song: Run, run, run! .... p. 36

Little Red Riding Hood .... p. 38

Song: Be Very Good! .... p. 44

Activities .... p. 45

Now, let's act it out! .... p. 57

Word List .... p. 63

a cape

beside

dark

a wood

This is Little Red Riding Hood.
She lives beside a big, dark wood.

bring a cake

grandma

sick

stop

Her mummy brings a cake one day.
"Grandma's very sick today.
Please take it to her now. Be good –
and don't stop in the big, dark wood!"

a wolf

bad

good

A wolf lives in the big, dark wood.
The wolf is bad. He isn't good.

look for

tasty

food

eat

tea

ask

over there.

far

an idea

pick flowers

a lovely day

run away

Now, the big bad wolf has got an idea.
"Pick some flowers for her, my dear!
Take your time, it's a lovely day!"
Then he quickly runs away.

Song: Red Riding Hood

Red Riding Hood, Red Riding Hood –
a little girl who's very good!

Chorus: Red coat, red shoes,
and a little red hood.
This is the story
of Red Riding Hood!

Grandma's very sick today.
Red Riding Hood is on her way!

Repeat Chorus

The big bad wolf is watching her.
He's got big teeth and lots of fur!

Repeat Chorus

She stops to pick some lovely flowers,
and stays in the wood for hours and hours!

Repeat Chorus

a house

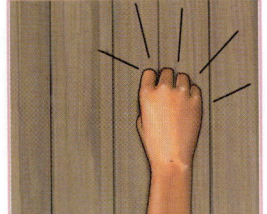
knock

ugly beautiful

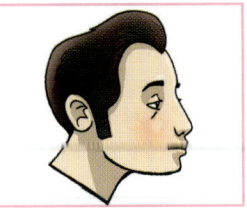
a head

hide

under

18

The wolf runs to Grandma's house in the wood.
"Knock, knock! It's me! Red Riding Hood!"
"Oh dear! That's the wolf's big, ugly head!
Where can I hide? Oh ...! Under my bed!"

walk into

see

a mouse

here

a room

The wolf walks into Grandma's house.
But all he sees is a little mouse!
"There's no tasty food here in this room!
But, Red Riding Hood is coming soon!"

Activities C-E

put on

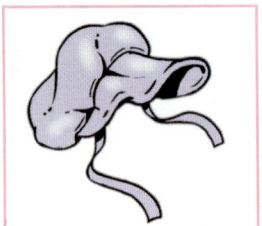
a nightcap

jump into

a bed

He puts a nightcap on his head and quickly jumps into Grandma's bed!

sit

And now Red Riding Hood is here.
"Hello! How are you, Grandma dear?"
"Come here, my dear, and sit by me!
Heehee! It's nearly time for tea!"

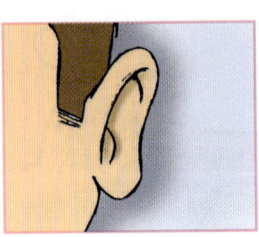
an ear

hear

"Grandma, what big ears you've got!"
"That's because I want to hear a lot!"

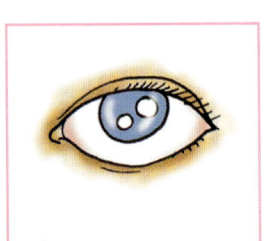
an eye

"And Grandma, what big eyes you've got!"
"That's because I want to see a lot!"

Activities F-G

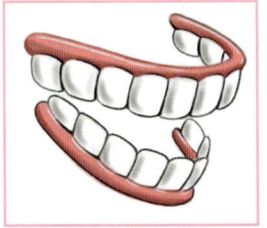

teeth

fall

bump

The big, bad wolf jumps out of bed.
But he falls and bumps his ugly head!

"I'm here, my dear. Let's run away!
The wolf can't have his food today!"

Song
Run, run, run!

The wolf is lying in Grandma's bed.
He's got a nightcap on his head!

Chorus: Run, run, run, Red Riding Hood!
Run with Grandma through the wood!

What big ears you've got, Grandma!
You can hear everything, near and far!

Repeat Chorus

What big eyes you've got, Grandma!
You can see everything, near and far!

Repeat Chorus

What big teeth you've got, Grandma!
You can eat everything, near and far!

Repeat Chorus

fast

through

wait

a gate

So Grandma and Red Riding Hood run very fast through the big, dark wood. Mummy's waiting at the gate. "Red Riding Hood, you're very late!"

a bump

And Mr Wolf still lives in the wood.
But the bump on his head has made him good!

Activities H-I

Song

Be Very Good!

Boys and girls,
be very good.
Don't go alone
in the big dark wood!

Chorus: Listen to your
mum and dad.
Listen to them.
Don't be bad!

Don't stop to talk
or say hello
to anybody
you don't know.

Repeat Chorus

ACTIVITIES

Activities for pages 4-11

A Look at the pictures and write the words.

0 ..little..   1 ....   2 ....   3 ....   4 ....

B Can you find these words in the puzzle?

~~wood~~
stop
look for
tea
good
eat
bring a cake
food
wolf
hood
beside

T	E	R	E	O	N	C	I	H	E	W
A	G	R	Y	F	Z	H	W	O	O	D
W	O	L	F	O	X	B	I	O	W	H
H	Q	O	W	O	E	R	S	D	R	A
T	G	O	O	D	E	D	T	O	S	E
H	T	K	N	B	E	S	I	D	E	E
E	D	F	E	P	D	A	S	T	O	P
T	S	O	E	R	O	E	F	E	K	R
S	B	R	I	N	G	A	C	A	K	E
O	S	H	T	A	K	T	A	B	A	S

45

Activities for pages 12-21

C Look and write.

0. <u>g r a n d m a</u> — m a d r a n g

1. _ _ _ _ _ _ _ _ — w o l f e r s

2. _ _ _ _ _ — m o r o

3. _ _ _ _ — a c k e

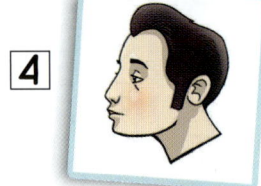
4. _ _ _ _ — d a e h

5. _ _ _ _ — d a e i

D Look at the pictures and add the missing letters to complete each word.

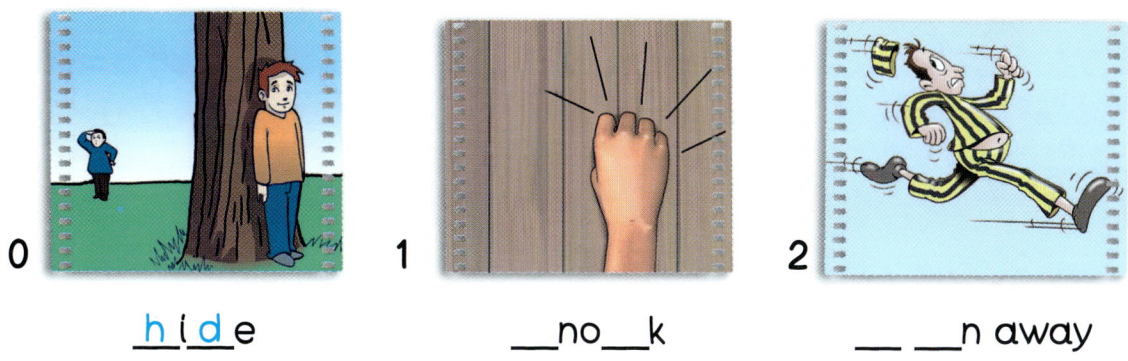

0 _h_ _i_ _d_ e

1 __no__k

2 __ __n away

3 __s__

4 __e__

5 __a__k into

6 __i__k

7 c__p__

E Look at the pictures and letters and write the words.

0

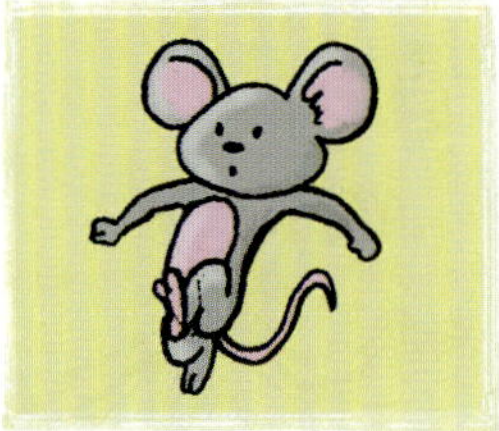

e s m o u

m o u s e

1

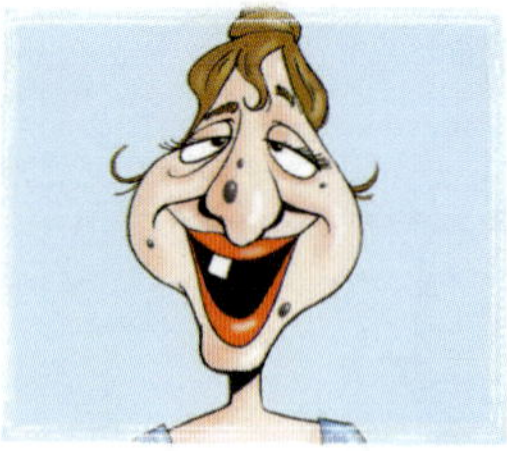

g y l u

_ _ _ _

2

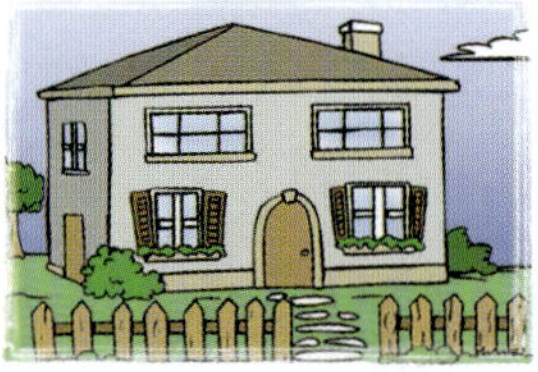

h u s e o

_ _ _ _ _

3

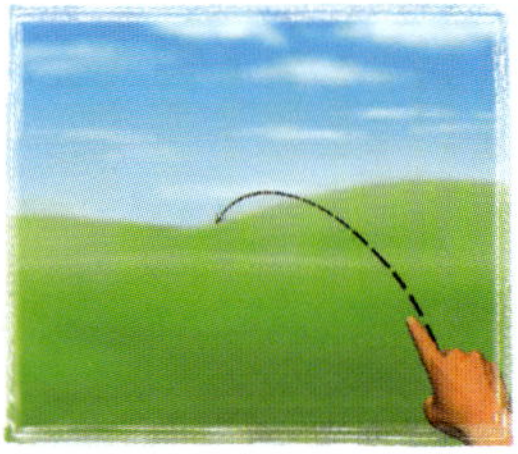

a r f

_ _ _

4

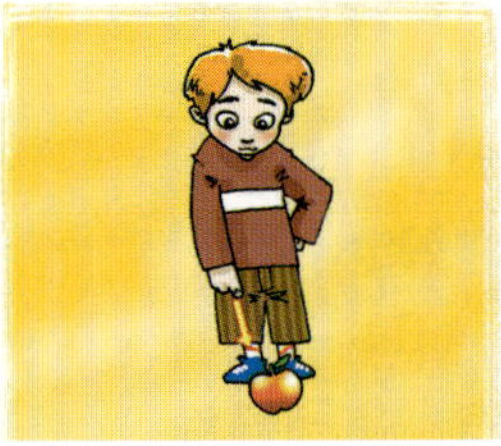

e h e r

_ _ _ _

5

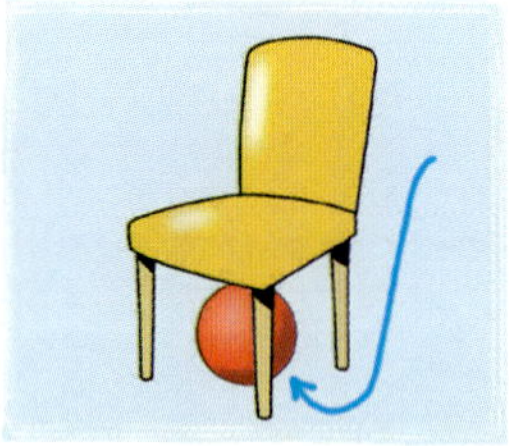

n r u e d

_ _ _ _ _

Activities for pages 22-29

F Look at the pictures and match them to the words.

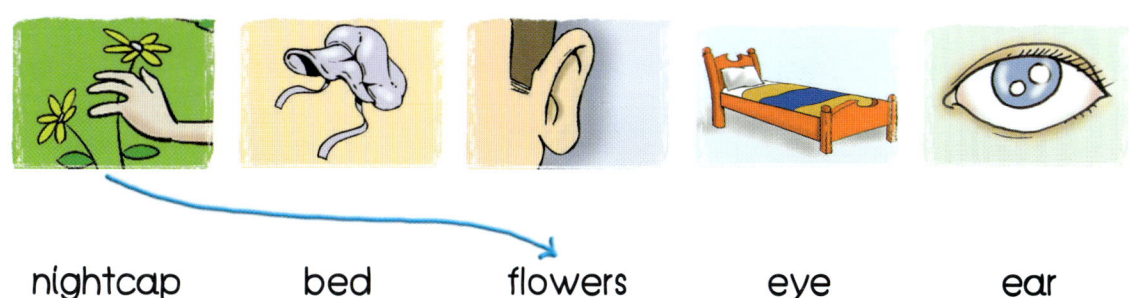

nightcap   bed   flowers   eye   ear

G Look at the pictures and circle the correct word.

0
a (sit)
b eat

1
a jump into
b walk into

2
a bring a cake
b put on

3
a ask
b run away

4
a hear
b see

5
a walk into
b eat

Activities for pages 30-43

H Look at the pictures and fill in the missing letters to find the secret words.

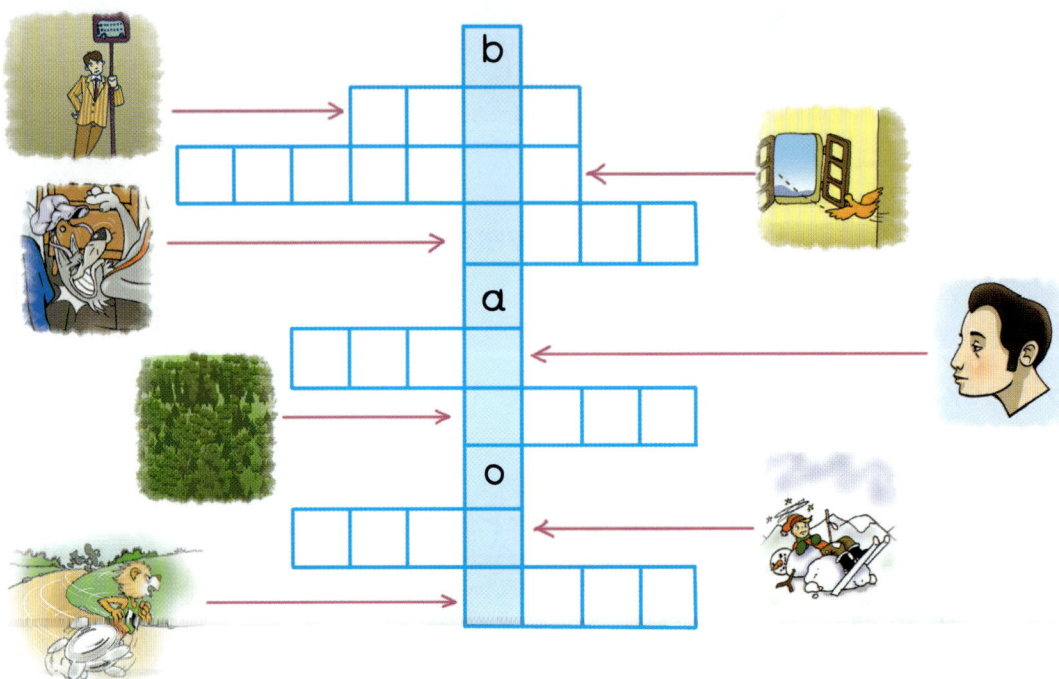

Secret words: _ _ _ _   _ _ _   _ _ _ _

I Look at the pictures and match them to the words in the box.

| a gate | teeth | a bump |

1 ....
2 ....
3 ....

Activities for the whole story

J Look at the alphabet key and write out words from the story.

a	b	c	d	e	f	g	h	i	j	k	l	m
8	21	9	23	11	10	3	5	12	18	22	14	25

n	o	p	q	r	s	t	u	v	w	x	y	z
24	16	17	4	26	19	20	6	13	2	7	15	1

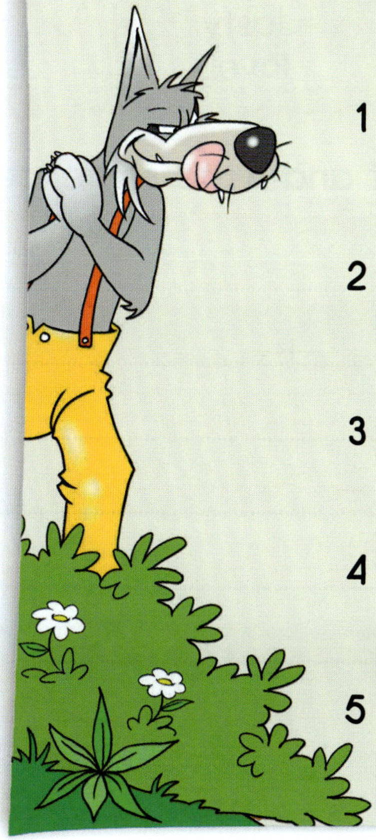

0 m o u s e
25 16 6 19 11

1 __ __ __ __   __ __ __ __ __
16 13 11 26   20 5 11 26 11

2 __ __ __ __ __ __ __ __
24 12 3 5 20 9 8 17

3 __ __ __ __
12 23 11 8

4 __ __ __   __ __ __ __
26 6 24   8 2 8 15

5 __ __ __ __ __
22 24 16 9 22

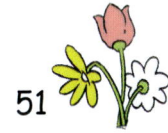

K   Look at the picture of the wolf.

bad   eyes   teeth
ugly   good   sick
little big   tasty
fast   ears   lovely

Now, find words about the wolf and write sentences.

0   The wolf is big.

00 The wolf has got big ears.

1   ....

2   ....

3   ....

4   ....

L a) Write the words.

b) Now, draw lines to match the words that rhyme!

M Who says it? Write **W** for the **Wolf**, **R** for **Red Riding Hood** and **G** for **Grandma**.

0 I'm looking for some tasty food. ....W........

1 She lives over there. It isn't far! ....

2 Come here, my dear, and sit by me! ....

3 Grandma, what big ears you've got! ....

4 Where can I hide? Oh ...! Under my bed! ....

5 I'm here, my dear. Let's run away! ....

6 I won't do it again, don't worry! ....

N Look at the pictures and read the sentences. Put a tick (✔) or a cross (✗).

0 This is a cake.

1 This is a bed.

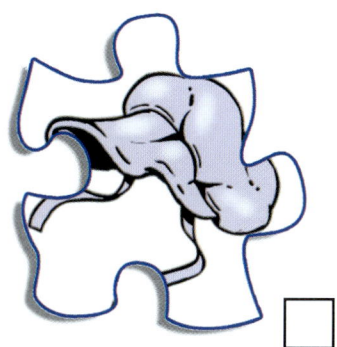

2 This is a nightcap.

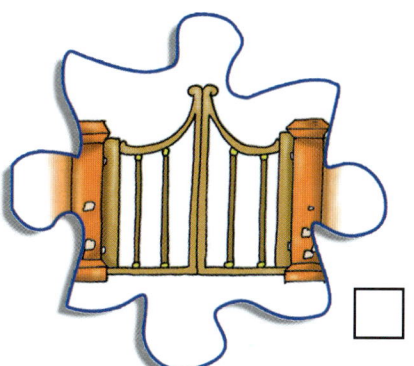

3 This is a gate.

4 This is a house.

5 This is an eye.

O Read the sentences and colour in Red Riding Hood.

Her cape is red.
Her dress is blue.
Her face is pink.
Her hair is orange.
Her flowers are red and green.
Her eyes are blue.
Her shoes are red.

▶ **Now, let's act it out!**

Actors: Red Riding Hood (RRH)
Mummy
Wolf
Grandma

Narrator(s): 1 or as many Ss as necessary, dressed as forest animals.

Scene 1

Narrator: This is Little Red Riding Hood.
She lives beside a big, dark wood.

Her mummy brings a cake one day.

Mummy: Grandma's very sick today.
Please take it to her now. Be good –
and don't stop in the big, dark wood!

Narrator: A wolf lives in the big, dark wood.
The wolf is bad. He isn't good.

Wolf: I'm looking for some tasty food.
I want to eat Red Riding Hood!
Here she comes! Let me see ...
Yummy, yummy! Time for tea!

Hello, Red Riding Hood, my dear!
Can I ask what you're doing here?

RRH: I'm going to see my poor grandma.
She lives over there. It isn't far!

Narrator: Now, the big, bad wolf has got an idea.

Wolf: Pick some flowers for her, my dear!
Take your time, it's a lovely day!

Narrator: Then he quickly runs away.

Song: Red Riding Hood

Red Riding Hood, Red Riding Hood –
a little girl who's very good!

Chorus: Red coat, red shoes,
and a little red hood.
This is the story
of Red Riding Hood!

Grandma's very sick today.
Red Riding Hood is on her way!

Repeat Chorus

The big bad wolf is watching her.
He's got big teeth and lots of fur!

Repeat Chorus

She stops to pick some lovely flowers,
and stays in the wood for hours and hours!

Repeat Chorus

Scene 2

Narrator: The wolf runs to grandma's house in the wood.

Wolf: Knock, knock! It's me! Red Riding Hood!

Grandma: Oh dear! That's the wolf's big, ugly head! Where can I hide? Oh ...! Under my bed!

Narrator: The wolf walks into Grandma's house. But all he sees is a little mouse!

Wolf: There's no tasty food here in this room! But, Red Riding Hood is coming soon!

Narrator: He puts a nightcap on his head and quickly jumps into Grandma's bed!

And now Red Riding Hood is here.

RRH: Hello! How are you, Grandma dear?

Wolf: Come here, my dear, and sit by me! Heehee! It's nearly time for tea!

RRH: Grandma, what big **ears** you've got!

Wolf: That's because I want to hear a lot!

RRH: And Grandma, what big **eyes** you've got!

Wolf: That's because I want to see a lot!

RRH: But Grandma, what big **teeth** you've got!

Wolf: That's because I want to **eat** a lot!

Narrator: The big, bad wolf jumps out of bed.
But he falls and bumps his ugly head!

Grandma: I'm here, my dear. Let's run away!
The wolf can't have his food today!

Song: Run, Run, Run!

The wolf is lying in Grandma's bed.
He's got a nightcap on his head!

Chorus: Run, run, run, Red Riding Hood!
Run with Grandma through the wood!

What big ears you've got, Grandma!
You can hear everything, near and far!

Repeat Chorus

What big eyes you've got, Grandma!
You can see everything, near and far!

Repeat Chorus

What big teeth you've got, Grandma!
You can eat everything, near and far!

Repeat Chorus

Scene 3

Narrator: So Grandma and Red Riding Hood run very fast through the big, dark wood. Mummy's waiting at the gate.

Mummy: Red Riding Hood, you're very late!

RRH: I'm sorry, Mummy. I'm really sorry! I won't do it again, don't worry!

Narrator: And Mr Wolf still lives in the wood. But the bump on his head has made him good!

Song: Be Very Good!

Boys and girls,
be very good.
Don't go alone
in the big dark wood!

Chorus: Listen to your
mum and dad.
Listen to them.
Don't be bad!

Don't stop to talk
or say hello
to anybody
you don't know.

Repeat Chorus

Props

Props	SCENE 1	SCENE 2	SCENE 3
basket	✓	✓	
cake wrapped in cloth	✓	✓	
flowers	✓	✓	✓

Word List

The words in colour are presented in the picture dictionary of the story.

ask
away
bad
beautiful
bed
beside
big
bring a cake
bump
cape
come
dark
day
dear
ear
eat
eye
fall
far
fast
food
gate
good
grandma

head
hear
hello
here
hide
hood
house
How are you?
idea
jump into
knock
late
let's
little
look for
lovely day
mouse
mummy
nearly
nightcap
now
over there
pick flowers
please

Word List

poor
put on
quickly
red
room
run away
see
sick
sit
some
soon
sorry
still
stop
take

tasty
tea
teeth
through
time
today
ugly
under
wait
walk into
want
wolf
wood
worry
yummy